Don't Talk with Your Mouth Full

Don't Talk with Your Mouth Full

100 Tips to Sign Language Sanity

Marie LaBozzetta Laurino, Ed.D.

abbott press®

A DIVISION OF WRITER'S DIGEST

Don't Talk with Your Mouth Full
100 Tips to Sign Language Sanity

ISBN: 978-1-4582-0336-6 (sc)
ISBN: 978-1-4582-0337-3 (e)

Library of Congress Control Number: 2012906978

Abbott Press books may be ordered through booksellers or by contacting:

Abbott Press
1663 Liberty Drive
Bloomington, IN 47403
www.abbottpress.com
Phone: 1-866-697-5310

Because of the dynamic nature of the Internet, any web addresses or links contained in this book may have changed since publication and may no longer be valid. The views expressed in this work are solely those of the author and do not necessarily reflect the views of the publisher, and the publisher hereby disclaims any responsibility for them.

Any people depicted in stock imagery provided by Thinkstock are models, and such images are being used for illustrative purposes only.

Certain stock imagery © Thinkstock.

Printed in the United States of America

Abbott Press rev. date:5/23/2012

To my family

No man is an island.
John Donne (1572-1631)

Preface

There are many personal and professional influences in my life responsible for molding me into the person I am today. These influences include people I've met, places I've visited, books I've read and experiences that are treasures in my life. Throughout my profession working with children and adults who are Deaf or hard of hearing, there have been people who have mentored me, guided me, critiqued and supported me through a long and wonderful journey.

As I sat and reflected on this journey, I thought about how overwhelming it was years ago learning about Deaf culture, American Sign Language, visiting Deaf clubs, and studying for my degrees, and interpreting certifications. I thought about how wonderful it would be to have a little book to introduce some of the dos and don'ts of the profession. How great it would be to be exposed to some facts to ease into the field of Deafness by learning tips that would last a lifetime. Hence, the birth of this unique little book, *Don't Talk With Your Mouth Full*. It focuses on sign language and Deaf culture.

In every culture, there are guidelines as to what is most appropriate, and what actions need to be avoided. Within these two covers, the reader will find cultural facts, sign language hints, helpful tips and a myriad of good sense suggestions. This book is a must have for those individuals starting out in a professional career related to deafness. It is a reminder to the vintage interpreter as well as the seasoned teacher and social worker of the wild and wonderful field in which they chose to enter. My journey has brought me to where I am today. Where will your journey take you?

Introduction

I walked into the room and saw 60 pairs of eyes eagerly staring my way. I was expected to say something profound, in sign language of course. I scanned the faces of the students, lifted my hands, and signed *Good Morning*. There wasn't a sound in the room. "How great is this?" I thought. If only all my audiences paid attention with such intensity and interest.

I was in the Media Center at a local middle school. In celebration of Deaf Awareness Month, I had been invited to talk to the sixth graders about sign language. This was my time to tell them all I knew, and I had 40 minutes to do it! I placed the index cards on the podium and proceeded to hold the interest of these students with fascinating stories of my many years in the field of Deafness. I supported the stories by using sign language and humor. Clearly, it was one of my most cherished moments. It gave me the opportunity to talk about my professional experiences working with Deaf and hard of hearing individuals, ranging in age from infancy to adulthood. I've had a long, diversified, and wonderful professional career, and it's not over. It has been and continues to be a good life!

But this book isn't about me. It's about you, and your journey to become a signer, a communicator, and maybe even an interpreter. It's about refining signing skills you may already possess or acquiring those you have yet to learn. This quaint little book can be your companion as you embark on your new adventure. Take the time to look inward and examine why you're going down this road. It's a journey with no end. There will be many side trips you'll experience, and many challenges you'll face. It's worth it! Along with acquiring this new language comes the opportunity to explore the history and culture of the Deaf population.

So let's get started! Contained in this publication are 99 tips to maintaining sign language sanity. There is no order of importance. You can go from one to 99 sequentially, or you can pick and choose at random. The choice is yours. INSERT YOUR OWN ONE HUNDREDTH TIP ON KEEPING YOUR SIGN LANGUAGE SANITY! Discuss them with friends. Add your own notes. Expand the list as you think of more. The possibilities are endless. When you are satisfied that you've covered all 100 tips, yours included, your work is still ahead of you to be the best signer you can be, in whatever arena you choose to use your new skill. You will be a shepherd of the language. Use this responsibility wisely. Good luck to you!

Don't forget to INSERT YOUR OWN ONE HUNDREDTH TIP ON KEEPING YOUR SIGN LANGUAGE SANITY! The 100th tip is YOURS. You have ownership of it, so make it a good one!

1. ***It's a language, not a game:***
   Sign Language is a complete language with its own conventions, reflective of the community from which it emerged. It has its own vocabulary, syntax and grammar.

2. ***Respect the culture:***
   If you respect the language, you'll respect the culture. A language does not exist in isolation. It is a reflection of the culture of its people.

3. ***It is not a cake-walk:***
   Sign language, like any language, requires study, usage and attention to detail. If you don't use it, you'll lose the ability to sign fluently. Stay current and stay on top of your lessons, always moving forward to become more skilled as a signer.

4. ***Practice, practice, practice:***
   As you're driving, think about how to sign words you see on billboards. Review the old and practice new signs and sign concepts. Listen to the radio and pick words for which you know the signs and visualize how you would say it. Learn a new sign each day.

5. ***Be crisp and clean with your signs:***
   Nobody likes a sloppy signer. Sloppy signing is like voiced mumbling. You can't be understood. Take the time to sign clearly and precisely. Speed will come later. Begin with accuracy.

6. ***Associate with Deaf individuals:***
   An excellent way to learn the language of sign is to associate with Deaf individuals, those who proudly boast of having sign as their native language. Watch as the

signing changes when they talk to student signers. See if you can see the difference in how they express themselves at a business meeting or at a social function. Can you identify which mode of sign communication they are using?

7. **Practice in a mirror:**
An excellent practice tool is looking in the mirror and signing to yourself. Your hands are facing in the proper outward direction so your *self* can read the signs, and you can correct any errors. See yourself as others see you. Are you graceful and accurate in your delivery? Self-critique your signing.

8. **Learn the language's history:**
In today's world of high speed technology, instant information is only a click away. Take the opportunity to learn the origin of American Sign Language. Research how it developed, when it reached our country, and who is credited with bringing it here. Take pride in learning the history of American Sign Language (ASL).

9. **Use sign concepts correctly:**
A sign concept is the expression of one word or several words in one sign that has a definite meaning. The concept should always be delivered accurately and concisely. Some examples are those signs specific to meetings. The motion is tabled. The word *tabled* would be signed as in suspending something, not the object table. I second that motion. The word *second* in this instance is signed with the index finger extended, and the thumb extended, with the other three fingers made into a fist. The hand makes an almost hook-like motion similar to the letter *J*. It is not the same as the second child in the row. Know the difference and use the correct sign concept.

10. Whatever you know, there's that much more you don't know:
You will never, ever know it all. Don't be a smarty-pants and strut your stuff thinking you're the best thing since sliced tomatoes! Acknowledge your accomplishments and continue to move forward. No one loves a Know-It-All.

11. Never correct a Deaf person's signs:
Rarely, is ASL someone's native language unless you're Deaf or related to deafness. If you question a Deaf person's sign, ask for clarification. It may be regional. Perhaps it is an old fashioned sign or slang. No matter what the reason for your belief that it is incorrect, it is acceptable to inquire but rude to assume you know better.

12. Don't talk with your mouth full:
In every culture, there are certain behaviors that are acceptable and others that are not. Learn the proper rules of etiquette in the Deaf community. How do you get someone's attention when you approach a Deaf individual? How do you get someone's attention in a crowded room? When is it appropriate to touch someone, and where? Please remember, don't talk with your mouth full!

13. Place signs in the correct position on your body:
When making a sign, one needs to be attentive to the shape of the hands, the relationship to the body, and the direction in which the sign is moving. Ultimately, all three of these factors must be in sync with each other in order to make the correct sign. If the hand configuration for *father* is on your chin, you're signing *mother*. Move it down to your chest, and you're saying *fine*. The sign cannot be almost right. It either is or it's not.

14. *Hearing individuals are more apt to confuse look-alike signs:*
Hearing individuals seem to confuse similar signs that don't have similar meanings. An example would be *meat* and *earth*. The signs are similar, but they are not the same, nor do they carry the same meaning.

15. *Deaf individuals are more apt to confuse similar meaning signs:*
Deaf individuals seem to confuse similar meaning signs that don't necessarily look anything alike. An example would be the signs for both the negative and positive connotation, *take advantage of.* One sign denotes negative as in *abusing the system,* while the other denotes positive as in *benefitting from.*

16. *Signs are regional within the United States:*
Florida, as are many other states in the United States, is a transient state. People visit, vacation and relocate from other parts of the USA. By knowing regional signs, we can take an educated guess as to which part of the country someone is from. This provides us with a diverse sign vocabulary and broadens our signing knowledge.

17. *Signs vary from Country to Country:*
Not all countries have a sign language that is compatible with American Sign Language. However, signing among various countries, no matter how diverse the signing may be, is still more understandable among its users than the voiced language. Because sign languages are so iconic, the signs often look like what they mean, and therefore, can be understood more easily.

18. Find a mentor:
An asset to any learning experience is to have a mentor. This mentor may be a professor, a Deaf acquaintance, a relative, or someone in the interpreting profession. Pick someone you can trust, who will be honest with you, and who knows the skill you are striving to learn. Don't pick someone who will support your poor signing habits. Keep your eye on the goal, and work with a mentor.

19. Don't partner with a Deaf lover for the experience:
An interpreter *wannabee* told me he was not getting along with his girlfriend, their relationship was over, and he wanted her to move out. He asked my advice on how to handle this situation. It seemed like a reasonable request for her to go, but he was having a hard time telling her to leave. She was Deaf. I told him that he would tell her to leave if she were hearing. There is no difference. He took her as his lover for all the wrong reasons.

20. American Sign Language is always changing:
If a language, any language, doesn't continually evolve, it becomes stagnant and dies. American Sign Language is an ever evolving language. It incorporates terminology and technology of today. ASL is as current and vibrant a language as it was in its infancy, even though it has changed dramatically.

21. Accept the various modes of sign communication:
Keep an open mind. Just because you prefer Signed English or Pidgin, doesn't mean everyone else supports that concept. I strongly support Total Communication, which is English word order, ASL concepts, and voicing while you're signing. Respect another's choice just as you want other individuals to respect yours.

22. *Own up to your signing errors:*
Don't make excuses for your mistakes. Own them and learn from them. They'll make you a better signer. We seem to remember our errors much more vividly than we do our successes!

23. *Laugh at yourself:*
Life is too short to take ourselves seriously. Take your work seriously, your education and your family commitments seriously, but don't take yourself seriously. Laughter can be a miraculous healer.

24. *Learn about technology and how it's used by the Deaf community:*
Years ago, those Deaf individuals who were fortunate to own a huge text telephone (TTY) had it hidden in the closet to avoid having it spotted by the phone company. Today, we have modern technology to draw Deaf and hard of hearing individuals into the mainstream of the hearing world. Take the time to learn how technology influences those who cannot hear and improves their world.

25. *Dream in Sign Language:*
Someday, when you least expect it, you'll make a notation in your diary: "Last night, I had a dream in sign language."

26. *A baby's signs are similar to baby talk:*
When a baby starts to speak, the words are close to the correct pronunciation. It takes practice and listening to others to perfect the speech patterns. This is also true with babies communicating in sign language. Their signs are approximations of the correct sign. With time, repetition, modeling and maturity, the correct signs will emerge. In the meantime, it's baby talk!

27. Sign Language is not exclusively for Deaf or hard of hearing persons:
Reaching outside of the Deaf community, we become aware of a myriad of reasons someone signs. It may be because a student is choosing sign language to satisfy his foreign language requirement. Perhaps, it is the chosen language of someone who is striving to become a sign language interpreter. Add to these reasons the fact that sign language is also used as a mode of communication for non-verbal children and adults.

28. Don't "eyes drop" if it is not appropriate:
Is it ever appropriate to *eyes drop* on someone else's conversation? Equate it with listening in on someone's conversation when you're not included, and it's really none of your business. If you're not supposed to be listening, then you're not supposed to be watching. Just because sign language is so visual, and you can see a conversation across the room, doesn't mean you should be looking. Give the participants in a signed interaction the same courtesy that you'd give those people involved in spoken conversation.

29. Babies learn to sign before they learn to speak:
Documentation has it that babies have signed as early as six months of age. The musculature to produce speech is more refined than the musculature needed to sign. Therefore, signing may exhibit itself before speech does.

30. A communicator is not an interpreter:
The commonality between an interpreter and a communicator in sign language is that they both use a manual means of presenting information. Both entities, however, are different and require different skills. A communicator is one who is skilled and poised in

conversation. An interpreter is one who transmits another's message with accuracy, timing and professionalism, and who may hold certification in a national interpreting organization.

31. *Sign Language as a foreign language is awesome:*
State colleges and universities offer sign language as a means to satisfy the requirements of a foreign language. It is also recognized and accepted as a foreign language in some community colleges and high schools.

32. *Moving closer to the Deaf signer does not guarantee comprehension:*
I remember moving my chair forward to be closer to a Deaf individual who was signing using the Rochester Method. He was speaking to a group of friends during an outdoor picnic. I thought that perhaps if I saw better, I'd understand more. It didn't make any difference! His speed and dexterity were far beyond my skill level. The Rochester Method comes from Rochester, NY. One fingerspells everything, with the hand beside the mouth while talking or mouthing the words.

33. *Respect the Deaf community:*
The Deaf community is a very proud community, many of whom are second and third generation Deaf. Do not judge, and do not criticize the beliefs and actions of the Deaf community. You may not understand why they do what they do, but always respect their right to do it. Please remember, that in the Deaf culture, deafness is not a disability.

34. Don't worry about national certification or state screening yet:
If you're just starting out, focus on improving your skill level and don't worry about earning national certification. That level of skill will come with time, practice, and interaction with the Deaf community. Certification is mandatory if your goal is to become an interpreter; it's optional if you're following the route of a communicator.

35. Is there a difference between Deaf and deaf?
The answer is *yes*, there is a difference between big D and little d. We use D to denote a culturally Deaf individual, one who is born Deaf, has been raised as a Deaf person and believes himself to be part of the Deaf community. The lower case d is used for someone who is not culturally deaf and who fits the description of one having a hearing loss.

36. Sign with music:
Signing with music has a myriad of positive effects. You can sing along and sign those words or concepts with which you're familiar. It's a great way to pace your practice signing by following the beat. As time goes on and your skills improve, you'll be signing more and more of the songs. It's also a wonderful way of incorporating your body language, facial expressions and signs into a total signing package. Besides, how can you sing, sign and not be happy?

37. Learn the history of the signs:
I have always found it easier to remember a sign when I know the history of it. How do you sign *gas*, as in petro? Your non-dominant *S* shaped hand is the tank and the dominant *A* shaped hand is the gas spout. The thumb of

11

the dominant hand goes into the non-dominant *S* hand as you would put gas in the car gas tank. Take the time to learn why signs are the way they are, and you'll be happy you did.

38. Remember to breathe:
When you become overwhelmed with your signing, remember to breathe! Never hold your breath while signing. You'll turn blue and someone will have to scrape you up off the floor!

39. There are many correct signs, but when it's wrong, it's wrong:
You may use one sign and see another sign used for the same expression. Often, there is more than one sign from which to choose. It could be an older sign, or a regional sign. However, if you realize the sign you are using is wrong, admit it and move on. There is nothing worse than attempting to rationalize why the incorrect sign you're using is right!

40. Eliminate the mouth clicking and tongue thrusts:
Many Deaf people make clicking sounds when they sign. They may even do tongue thrusts. Monitor yourself to prevent these types of actions. Use your monitoring devices, your ears. Remember, you are not Deaf.

41. Identify at least 10 famous Deaf individuals:
Can you name 10 famous Deaf individuals? Can you name 10 individuals who are well known in the field of Deafness? Invest time in learning about those who were trail blazers. Research Deaf individuals who made an impact on the lives of those who came after them. Dazzle your friends with your new found knowledge. They'll be impressed!

42. *Learn about the football huddle:*
Do you know that the Deaf football team is credited for the first football huddle, dating as far back as 1880 at Gallaudet College in Washington, D.C.?

43. *ABCs are important, and...:*
Learning the alphabet is critically important to becoming a good signer. The finger spelling Rochester Method is not as popular as it used to be, but finger spelling still has a place in the Deaf community. Don't be afraid to spell to children, either. They learn the configuration of the finger spelled word the same way they learn the configuration of the written word. Please do not create your own signs. It only causes confusion, and few people know what you're saying. If you don't know the sign, find out what it is. If there isn't a sign for what you need to identify, spell it.

44. *Knowing sign language has some great benefits:*
There are some great advantages to knowing sign language besides the fact that it is a beautiful language. Having laryngitis doesn't slow you down. You can chat at a distance. Noisy environments don't stop you from communicating. You can have a private conversation without others knowing what you're saying. What would you say are some great benefits of knowing sign language?

45. *Visit the State School for the Deaf in your area:*
Do you know the location of the State School for the Deaf in your state? Take time to locate it. A tour of the school will teach you a great deal about what the school has to offer its students. The Florida School for the Deaf and Blind (FSDB) is located in northeast Florida in a city named St. Augustine.

46. *Enjoy the journey:*
Learning sign language is a journey. You will never be able to say that you're done and that you've learned all you can learn. The language is constantly changing. You will spend your life learning new signs to stay current in today's world. Enjoy the journey. It's a wonderful experience!

47. *Various specialty groups have signs specific to that field, such as medicine, law, religion, etc.:*
Do you have a special interest in learning sign language? There are specific sign characteristics and vocabulary in the fields of medicine, law, science, religion, and other fields of study.

48. *Why do you want to become a signer?*
Look inwardly and think deeply as to why you want to learn sign language. Be sure it is for the right reason. If you feel maternal or paternal instincts towards the Deaf community, or you're out to save someone, you're doing it for all the wrong reasons. If you consider yourself a savior and this is your mission, don't. Too many people do!

49. *What did you just say?*
I know someone who used to panic every time she saw someone signing a *wh* word. Why? Because, she knew it required a response. (*Who, What, Where, When, Why*). By the time it was necessary for her to answer, she was so stressed that she missed the whole passage. You can always ask for clarification. It's not the end of the world if you miss something. Oftentimes, contextual clues will get you back on track.

50. *Take your time and learn it right the first time*:
Learning a sign incorrectly and practicing it the wrong way only perpetuates the error. If you're vigilant and learn the sign the right way, you don't have to relearn it later. The signs for *again* and *against* are often signed incorrectly. Look them up. Are you signing them correctly? Another common mistake is confusing the term *late* with the sign for *later*.

51. *If a consumer is mentally ill, believe what you see*:
Working with mentally ill consumers who are Deaf, is a challenge. They may tell you what their reality is, but it doesn't sound right to you. You'll doubt you're seeing what you think you see. When I was in Puerto Rico, a Deaf tourist told me that aliens had stolen his mother and father and took them up in a flying saucer. At a mental health facility in the states, a patient told me she was a doctor and was waiting to perform surgery.

52. *A Deaf person will slur his signing when coming out of anesthesia*:
Think of someone you know who was attempting to speak post-surgery in the recovery room at a hospital. The verbiage didn't make sense and it was hard to understand. Apply that same idea to a Deaf individual. His signing is slurred and oftentimes doesn't make sense and is difficult to understand.

53. *CODA means Child of Deaf Adults*:
Children of Deaf adults are usually native signers. They sign before they speak. Many Deaf individuals can identify a CODA by the CODA's signing ability.

54. Sign Language is a beautifully artistic method of communicating:
Did you ever think about sign language being functional and beautiful? Think of it as hands, gracefully painting messages in the air.

55. Did you say what you mean, and mean what you said?
The message delivery always goes back to accuracy. Communication has a sender, a receiver and the message being relayed. If there is a breakdown in any of these three components, the message is tainted.

56. Body language and the delivered message should be in sync:
Your body language, facial expressions and the message should all deliver the same concept. Would you be giggling if you were telling someone some sad news? Would you look stern if you were spreading the word that you just aced a test? Keep your body language in sync with the message you're delivering.

57. How many ways can you sign the meaning of the word "run"?
Give this game a try. Write down all the ways the word *run* is used. Now, sign the various meanings of the word *run*. Don't forget to do it conceptually. I'll start you off with one example: John Doe is running for the office of City Comptroller.

58. What does confidentiality mean to you?
The Registry of Interpreters for the Deaf, Inc. *Code of Professional Conduct* (2005) contains seven tenets. Tenet one states: "Interpreters adhere to standards of confidential communication." Whether you're a signer or an interpreter, start early to respect others. As an

interpreter, you are mandated to follow the *Code of Professional Conduct*. If you're a communicator, I recommend it.

59. Signing can be dangerous!
You're trying to get a Deaf person's attention by standing on a chair. A Deaf friend wants to say something to you as you're standing in the middle of the parking lot, and your attention is on your friend. You get deeply involved in a conversation, your hands are too close to the object beside you, and you hit it. Deaf individuals make better use of their vision than hearing people. They don't see better but they are more aware of their surroundings. Be sure that *you* pay attention to *your* surroundings.

60. Using English idiomatic expressions is a WOW!
Here is some food for thought. How would you sign *It's Raining Cats and Dogs*, or *Throw Your Hat into the Ring*? Would you sign these idioms word for word or conceptually? What exactly do they mean? There are no cats or dogs, no hat or ring. Signing idioms can be a challenge. I was interpreting at a business meeting when a presenter used the expression, "*A duck is a duck is a duck. If it looks like a duck and smells like a duck, then it is a duck.*" Would you interpret it or transliterate it?

61. Growing up CODA in a hearing world:
Jerry B. Crittenden, Ph.D., contributes the following information about growing up hearing in a Deaf family, a CODA, a child of Deaf adults (2011). It is with great appreciation and respect for Dr. Crittenden that I include his complete passage.

About this CODA - my recall is that the growing up stages of my life were filled mainly with no thought about my parent's deafness. Inside the home we were a family who used sign to communicate. Outside I was my family's interpreter and my friends there were easily spoken to and with. It was not until I was an adult and head of my family that I noticed things like more conversation at meals and being able to communicate around corners or from room to room. And in the dark being able to speak rather than finding my parent's hands to sign and fingerspell into. I recall my first and only CODA meeting during which I heard people stand and say awful things about their deaf parents and their feelings of disgust. I was totally angry because my childhood memories are filled with the love of my parents and the blessing given me to communicate with beautiful hands. It is ASL now but it will always be the "sign" to me. Use what you wish, I never thought about being different because I was a CODA, for that matter, the whole idea never occurred to me! I was living comfortably in two worlds where in one I used my hands to speak, and in the other I used my mouth.

62. Excuse me. Are you Deaf?

Do you assume that because people are Deaf you can walk up and start talking to them? Do you have a right to enter their personal space because you can sign and so can they? It depends. Some Deaf individuals welcome the company, others do not. Make a judgment call based on the situation. In a very public location at the town square in San Jose', Costa Rica, I walked up to a group of young Deaf adults and introduced myself. We had a wonderful conversation, mostly about my coming from the States. Because I was going into their territory, I hesitated to approaching the group. Finally, I decided to talk with them because it was a very public area. I'm glad I did.

63. *Deaf speech may be challenging*:
If you are a hearing person, your ears monitor your speech. Not so with Deaf individuals. They cannot monitor what they say. At times, the pronunciation or the emphasis on a syllable may be incorrect. If you do not understand what a Deaf person is saying, ask what the topic of conversation is about to draw your focus towards that specific area.

64. *Can you identify parts of the body for certain categories of signs?*
Do you know that certain parts of the anatomy are where certain signs are placed? Male signs, such as uncle, father, grandfather, male cousin, brother and boy are placed on the upper part of the head. Female signs for aunt, mother, grandmother, female cousin, sister and girl are placed on the lower part of the face. Feeling and emotion signs are on the torso. These would include some signs such as happy, agitated, excited, depressed, fine, etc.

65. *Lag time! Help, I can't think of how to say it!*
Lag time is usually applied to an interpreter who needs to listen to the spoken word and signs a few seconds after the speaker. However, for those who are not interpreters, there are some signers who can't remember the sign fast enough to continue the conversation. Don't panic. It happens to us all. I compare it to having writer's block. The information is in our head, but we just don't seem to be able to retrieve it. Try it this way. You can ask the person to whom you're speaking for help. Explain in a sentence or two what you're trying to say. He may be able to feed you the sign. Another way of getting through these blocks is to use the opposite with negation. An example would be that you want to say it is foggy out, but you don't know how. Instead, say it is not clear. Give it a try.

66. *Finger spelling isn't always the answer*:
You may find yourself in a situation when there are no legitimate signs for what you're trying to say, and the receiver is having difficulty understanding you. You may think that signing isn't working so you switch to finger spelling. You may need to think again. Although finger spelling plays an important part in American Sign Language, it may not be the answer. Total Communication uses whatever is necessary to get the message from the sender to the receiver. This may include body language, drawings, signing, voicing and even acting out. Be creative when signing and finger spelling aren't enough.

67. *Flying fingers and happy hands can be yours*:
Hard work and perseverance will pay off with your signing. You'll feel more confident, sign more smoothly, and you'll want to continue on this marvelous journey. Make a DVD of yourself, and also watch yourself sign in a mirror. Compare the DVDs that are made one or two months apart. This is wonderful feedback as to how you're progressing.

68. *Playing with words and signs can be fun*:
There are some individuals in the interpreting profession who are just plain funny when they start playing word games with sign. I won't publish any names, but you'll learn soon enough who they are if you don't already know. They can change an entire song into sign language that is not conceptually correct and you'll be rolling on the floor with laughter. Even one-liners are hilarious. Have a nice *weekend* becomes have a nice *weak rear-end*. The word *comfortable* becomes *come-for-table*. The possibilities are endless!

69. *So you think you can sign:*
How wonderful! You are finding a confidence that will be a great support as you continue on your journey. Take the time to recognize your accomplishments. It's okay to pat yourself on the back and smile! You worked for it.

70. *Learning from a book just isn't enough:*
Learning to sign from a book augments learning by direct contact with other humans. It is not sufficient to learn the language exclusively from a text. The written words and the pictures are not three dimensional. Trying to follow the arrows that denote movement is almost impossible. Partner with another student, mingle with the Deaf community, watch DVDs, surf the web, and practice, practice, practice. Keep the books but don't make them the only place to go, excluding all other means of learning sign language.

71. *Children have a signing mode all their own:*
It is amazing to watch Deaf children sign. They are so comfortable and relaxed in their native language. Many children sign rather large signs that are approximations of correct signing. However, they progress at a rapid pace, and develop into beautiful communicators of a wonderful language.

72. *Did you know that American Sign Language came from France?*
Thomas Hopkins Gallaudet, a Protestant minister, met Laurent Clerc in London and traveled to France to visit the school for the deaf where Clerc was a student. The year was 1815. Gallaudet convinced Clerc to return with him to Connecticut and become a teacher for the deaf. Gallaudet and Clerc opened the Connecticut Asylum for the Education and Instruction of Deaf and Dumb

Persons in April 1817, the institution that is now called American School for the Deaf. It was at this school that a variety of influences would intermingle and become what is now known as American Sign Language.

73. *Are you a lefty or a righty?*

When signing, your dominant hand does most of the action. Your non-dominant hand is there to assist when you're using a two handed sign, each hand performing a different movement. This is evident with the signs for week and month. The signs for box and book use both hands in the same manner to complete the signs. If your teacher has the opposite hand dominance than you, it is easier to learn the signs because you're looking at a mirror image.

74. *Syntax, what, huh, what are you talking about?*

In American Sign Language (ASL), as in any formal language, there are rules and these rules include the structure of sentences. In ASL, the verb is followed by the object and the object is followed by the subject, for example, *go store me*. The adjectives describe the noun or pronoun and are placed after them, as in *house big yellow*. These are just two examples of ASL sentence syntax. You'll learn more as you gain more skills.

75. *Five fingers, two hands and far too many signs to count:*

Isn't it amazing what we can do with moving our hands! We show a language with innuendoes, tense, intensity, structure, and so much more. You'll be pleasantly surprised how many signs you'll learn in a relatively short period of time. Take those signs and make sentences. Make a video of yourself and watch it. Before you know it, your list of signs will be longer than you imagined, and it is all accomplished with two hands and ten little fingers.

76. Be prepared to screw up!

There will be times when you'll wonder what you're doing learning sign language. Nothing seems to be going right. You're using the wrong sign or sign concept. Be prepared for this. We learn as much from our mistakes as we do from our successes, and sometimes more!

77. Know your limitations:

Sometimes, in our enthusiasm we jump in "...where angels dare not tread", and we find ourselves in a situation where we should never be. Sometimes, in our hearts we want to help or assist. Be cautious. Don't place yourself in a position where your lack of signing experience and expertise can jeopardize the situation for others. A situation faux pas would be when a new interpreter or signer relays a message to a Deaf individual but, because of lack of skill and experience, the message is not relayed completely, accurately or in its entirety. Read the Registry of Interpreters for the Deaf, Inc. Code of Professional Conduct at www.rid.org to learn more.

78. Life is just a bowl of cherries:

I've spoken about not taking yourself too seriously. This may entail having a good laugh at yourself, either by yourself or with a friend. One of my funniest moments was when I was platform interpreting for a community meeting. My feet fell asleep, and when it was time to switch interpreters, I could barely walk as we made the exchange. As I stumbled off the stage, the presenter made mention that I looked like I was walking on egg shells. His intentions were to make light of the fact that I was struggling. We all laughed, including the audience!

79. *Never discount the skill and expertise of recognized leaders:*
Drawing on the skills and expertise of others is a great way to learn and grow. Recognized leaders in the fields of interpreting and Deafness are rich and fertile sources of information. Someone who was active in this profession and may now be retired has stories of what was that are fascinating and a part of history. Tap into it.

80. *Don't listen to everyone:*
Listening to everyone tell you what to do and how to do it will make you crazy. Listen to only those who know. Be selective. A mentor will provide you with valuable critique.

81. *Did I just curse?*
OMG! What did I just say? Like a spoken language, we may confuse words or signs with other words or signs. This can get us into trouble or just give us a good laugh. Has this happened to you yet?

82. *Don't be a chicken. Go ahead. Try it:*
I remember the very first time I signed to a Deaf person. I thought I was going to pass out. My hands were shaking, my knees were knocking and I forgot how to spell my first name! I lived to face another day, and so will you. Go ahead and take the first step in communicating in sign language.

83. *Counting? Face your hands towards those to whom you are signing:*
Many new signers have a tendency to look at their hand when they count. Turn your hand outward. Look at the back of the palm. Sign to the person in front of you, not to yourself. Numbers 11 through 15 have the back of the hand facing out.

84. *Keep the wind at your back, but not the sun:*
If the sun is at your back while you're signing, then the Deaf individual is looking into the sun and sees nothing more than the outline of your body. Never position yourself with the sun, a light or a window at your back. You want to be seen.

85. *Never, never, never give up!*
You'll have your good days, and there will be others that are not so good. At times, you'll doubt your progress. Never give up! Each day will bring you closer to meeting your goal of becoming a top notch signer.

86. *What's in a name sign?*
Name signs are very personal. Usually, the sign lends itself to a specific characteristic of the individual. My name sign is formed by *M* outlining what would be a scoop neck blouse. It was given to me by a Deaf lady who said I always wore shirts that have a scoop neckline. What unique trait or characteristic do you have that would lend itself to your name sign?

87. *Chances are, you're not a native signer:*
Members of the Deaf community have the skill to identify you as a native signer or not. Often times, Children of Deaf Adults (CODAS) are taken to be Deaf because of their signing skills. They were raised in a Deaf home, by Deaf parents, and their native language is sign language. Their sign delivery is different enough to be identified as a native language and not a learned language.

88. *You used what sign for what?*
Others may question why you're using a specific sign. If you're a newbie signer, you may be using an incorrect concept. As an interpreter, you may be hearing what wasn't

said. Perhaps the passage was about a *candy date*, and you heard *candidate*. These are all challenges that may slow you down, but you'll get through them. Keep plugging along. They are only bumps in the road.

89. *Think "context" when receiving or expressing signs*:
It always helps to know the topic that you'll be talking about. It gives you the luxury of focusing on vocabulary specific to that topic in both expressive and receptive signing. I refer to it as having a hook on which to hang your hat.

90. *Religious signing is quite unique:*
The vocabulary of religious signing is significantly different than general signing. Additionally, the words have meanings that are specific to that religion. Each religion has its own terminology and worship passages. An example of this would be that if you're interpreting in a synagogue, you won't need to know how to sign the *Lord's Prayer*. The ritual of the service is significant also, so before you volunteer to sign in your place of workshop, know what is expected of you, and practice, practice, practice.

91. *Remember the past, the present and the future:*
Although sign does not express a tense as speech does, it does, nevertheless, express tenses. There is the past behind us, the present directly in front of our body, and the future, which is noted by holding one hand sideways and motioning it forward. This will establish a time frame as you tell your story.

92. Sign language idioms are what they are, nothing more, nothing less:

One of the most commonly used idioms among new signers is signing *the train left*. What it really means is that it's too late, you missed your opportunity. If you don't know the idiom, it doesn't make sense. Like most idioms, both hearing and deaf, they are what they are.

93. Sign language is an "air" language:

Sign language is not a written language, although many individuals throughout the years have attempted to print the manual alphabet or create symbols to express signing. It is an air language. Once it is signed, it is gone. You can no longer see it, feel it, carry it around with you or listen to it. While it is in its present state of motion, sign language is artistic, it's graceful and it's air poetry.

94. What did you think you saw her say?

We oftentimes go into a conversation with a preconceived notion of what will be said. Signing is no different. Beware! If you latch onto a sign you think you saw, you may build the entire story around something that was never there. A sign language student told me her friend signed to her that she and her boyfriend didn't get out of bed for three days. NOT! Her boyfriend bought new contact lenses and didn't take them out for three days.

95. Investigate sign language and sign language related websites:

While you're diligently working to improve your signing skills, don't forget to nourish other parts of this adventure in sign language. Stay current with professional memberships, periodicals, website information, Deaf community news and any other means by which you can add to your professional growth and development.

96. *Beware of Deaf jokes:*
Deaf jokes are best told by Deaf people to Deaf people. That doesn't mean we can't learn to appreciate them. Deaf jokes are just different. I was at an Evening of Deaf Comedy. The featured stand-up comic did not present with an interpreter. All the guests knew this before purchasing tickets. The room was packed with Deaf participants, sign language interpreters, ASL students, CODAS and others. It was remarkable to listen to the wave of laughter after each joke. It started with the Deaf individuals and CODAS, followed by the interpreters. The ASL students either didn't get the joke or had a lag time that was significantly noticeable. If you haven't experienced it, you need to go!

97. *Avoid the dangers of comparing your learning skills with others:*
Don't worry about how others are progressing. Be in competition with yourself, not others. Everyone learns at his own pace. It is better to learn, retain, and improve than worry about what someone else is doing.

98. *Respect Deaf Pride:*
According to Jack Gannon (1981), the decade of the 1970s brought us more awareness and understanding of the Deaf community. It was a time of increased interest in sign language, passage of legislation that benefitted Deaf individuals and more Deaf people advocating for their rights.

99. *Learn about Gallaudet College:*
In 1954, an Act of Congress changed the corporate name of the Columbia Institution for the Deaf to Gallaudet College. It is located in Washington, D. C., and is an outstanding liberal arts college for Deaf students. However, its enrolled students are eclectic in their hearing abilities, ranging from profoundly deaf to normal hearing.

100. PLACE YOUR OWN PERSONAL ONE HUNDREDTH TIP HERE!

_____

_____

_____

_____

_____

_____

If you've made it this far, pat yourself on the back, sit back and relax. You deserve a break! Okay, that's long enough. Now get busy refining your skills. Congratulations from me to you!

Remember, the 100th tip is yours. You have ownership of it, so make it a good one!

Conclusion

Sign language is a language with syntax, conventions, tense, and idioms, to mention just a few components of the language. These are characteristics of all languages. The words may sound familiar to you, but remember the uniqueness of this language. It is not spoken. It is not written. It is an air language. When a message is communicated in sign language, it is not heard. When a story is told, the words and concepts are not captured. No one hears what is said yet everyone sees the beautiful picture unfold in American Sign Language. The conversations are not captured on a CD, and they are not preserved on paper. But, with today's technology, we can reach across the neighborhood or around the world to communicate in sign. DVDs, video relay, Skype, and cell phones are just a few ways to keep in touch with our Deaf or hard of hearing professionals, friends and family.

Sign language is a reflection of the Deaf culture. Sign language is not a stagnant language. It is continually changing and meeting the demands of the scientific, educational and technical worlds. It reflects our times. It is regional and oftentimes reveals a person's country of origin by the signs used to express oneself. Respect the language and you'll respect the culture. Respect the culture and you'll respect the language. They cannot and will not be separated as individual entities.

Should you pursue a career in the field of Deafness, or learn sign language for your personal growth and development, take the time to learn it correctly. Practice, practice and practice. Sign conceptually. Differentiate between those words that sound the same but have different meanings. Spend time with those who will mentor you and from whom you will learn. Become involved in the Deaf community.

My wish for each and every one of you, is that you will find passion and joy in learning sign language.

About the Author

Marie LaBozzetta Laurino, Ed.D. received her Masters of Science Degree in Aural Rehabilitation from the University of South Florida, and her Doctorate in Education from Argosy University. She holds national certification from the Registry of Interpreters for the Deaf, Inc., and a State of Florida teaching certification for Deaf and hard of hearing students, birth to 22 years of age .

Dr. Laurino worked for the Friends of the Deaf Service Center, Inc., a not-for-profit agency serving Deaf and hard of hearing children and adults in Pinellas County, Florida, as an interpreter, a program director and as the assistant executive director. She chaired committees on both the National and Florida Registry of Interpreters for the Deaf, Inc., and held the office of Chairman of the Florida Council for the Hearing Impaired and the Treasurer for the Deaf Service Center Association, Inc. Dr. Laurino is currently employed by the District School Board of Pasco County, Florida as a Resource Teacher for Deaf and hard of hearing students.

Dr. Laurino's research on characteristics of effective sign language interpreters is captured on DVDs and available to the public. They include interviews with Icons in the field of Deafness. These Icons, both Deaf and hearing, share their expertise on the role of the interpreter, confidentiality, preferred characteristics of interpreters, interpreter preparedness and more. The material addresses both educational and community interpreting. The interviews were conducted live in California at the National Center on Deafness at CSUN, in Arkansas at the University of Arkansas at Little Rock, in Florida at the Florida State School for the Deaf and Blind located in St. Augustine, and at private facilities. Each interview is interpreted by Jerry L. Conner, RID certified, Florida.

Dr. Laurino lives in Pasco County, Florida since 1976.

Resources

Florida Registry of Interpreters for the Deaf, Inc.
P.O.Box 4500
Tampa, Florida 33677
904.419.3743
FRIDCentral.org

National Registry of Interpreters for the Deaf, Inc.
333 Commerce Street
Alexandria, Virginia 22314
Telephone: 703.838.0030
TDD: 703.838.0459
RID.Org

Florida School for the Deaf and the Blind
207 N. San Marco Avenue
St. Augustine, Florida 32084
1.800.344.3732
VP 904.201.4557
FSDB.k12.fl.us

Florida Association of the Deaf, Inc.
7852 Mansfield Hollow Road
Delray Beach, Florida 33446.3317
FADcentral.org

National Association of the Deaf, Inc.
NAD.org

Alexander Graham Bell Association for the Deaf and Hard of Hearing
AGBell.org

Gallaudet University
800 Florida Avenue, NE
Washington, DC 20002-3695

Gallaudet.edu

NOTES

Printed in the United States
By Bookmasters